Peppi Puffin to the Rescue

I0409847

by Donna Lewis

William R. Parks
Stanwrite@aol.com

www.wrparks.com

Special thanks to:
Becki Peden and Doris Rapp
for help with photo selection.

This book is dedicated to all brave rescuers of marine animals.

Copyright © 2013 by Donna Lewis

Library of Congress Control Number: 2013912420

PEPPI PUFFIN TO THE RESCUE

Each morning at sunrise over the ocean,
the sun comes up pale and shy,
just a faint gleam
where water meets sky.
It begins to glow with reaching light
until the sun peeks out,
yellow-orange and bright.

It climbs up the sky
to announce a new day
in the bird-covered islands
that stand in the bay.

All over the islands
when each morning breaks,
you can see gulls and
puffins and kittiwakes.

One bird looked at the water below,
as waves bobbed
up and down
with the ocean's steady flow.

 He stretched his short neck
and gazed at the sky.
"What a beautiful day!" he exclaimed.
"How happy am I!"

He sang to himself
as he greeted the day
there by the cold waters
of an Atlantic Bay.

"I'm Peppi Puffin, an Atlantic puffin,
We're called 'The Clowns of the Sea',
I'm a happy, happy puffin,
and so very glad to be me."

Peppi's tummy was empty.
"Time to eat. Look out be-lo-ow!
A flip of my tail, head down,
toward the bottom I go.

Watch me dive and swim.
I'm slim and trim.
Under the water I go.
Look out be-lo-ow!"

Peppi swam here and there
in search of his meal,
darting about
like a swift moving seal.

To the back of his mouth
he tucked in each fish,
pushing them in
like filling a dish.

His mouth was soon full,
so back to the top,
he broke the surface
with a flip and a flop.

With a satisfied sigh,
he began to munch
as he sat on the water
to enjoy his lunch.

Oh-h, all these fishes
are so very delicious.
Yum, yummy,"
Peppi hummed as each bite
slid down into his tummy.

"Am I full?
Have I had enough?
I mustn't get fat
like a powder puff.

If I eat too much,
I cannot fly,
but just sit on the waves
and gaze at the sky."

Peppi thought for a moment
there near the shore.
"Um-m -m, maybe dessert?
Just one or two more?"

Peppi Puffin squawked happily.
"Here I go again. Bottoms up!
Look at me, look at me.
Here I go down deep in the sea."

Peppi bobbed up like a cork
on the waves of the bay.
Soon all his breakfast was gone
and the sun warmed the day.

On a nearby wall
sat a quiet seagull
Peppi watched as he floated
feeling sleepy and full.

SWISH!
SWOOSH!
SPLASH!

A huge wall of water
woke Peppi with a start.
"Help, help!" he yelled,
"The ocean is falling apart.

What has happened?
A tidal wave? An earthquake?"
Peppi was so scared
he began to shiver and shake.

More water came gushing down.
"Help, oh, help!
I am going to drown!"

Peppi Puffin dived below the surface
where he could get away fast.
"I must escape
before the next blast."

Then he saw in the water
one of the biggest animals alive.
It swept past, just a blur,
in a quick, shallow dive.

"A whale!" exclaimed Peppi.
"A creature so strong,
but what on earth
can possibly be wrong?"

Deep in the water,
the puffin sped away.
"Oh, me, oh, my.
What an exciting day!"

The whale suddenly rose
in a towering breach,
leaping as high
as it could possibly reach.

It held still for an instant,
then with a splash,
over it tumbled
with a deafening crash.

A twist and a turn
of its powerful tail,
showed the awesome power
of the humpback whale.

"Oh, dear, oh dear," moaned Peppi.
"Oh, dearie dear.
That whale is in very
great trouble, I fear."

He swam closer
and began to shout.
"Hey, Mister Whale, be still.
Stop leaping about.

I can't come any nearer
with all that thrashing.
Do be quiet.
Stop so much splashing.

Be calm and don't
make such a to-do.
I will come over and
try to help you."

"You puny puffin,
help a whale that is strong?
Leave me alone.
But I'll tell you what's wrong.

I will tell you why
I'm in such a twiddle.
A rope is looped
tight around my middle.

One end is wrapped twice
around my right flipper.
What I need is someone
with a very sharp clipper."

Up leaped the whale again
with a splash,
then slapped the hard surface
with another loud crash.

It knocked poor Peppi
straight up toward the sky,
twisting and turning
as the world whirled by.

He yelled at the whale
as he fell back down,
and glared at it
with a ferocious frown.

"STOP THAT!
You'll make the rope tighter.
I know you are strong
and you're a good fighter,"
he yelled with a yelp,
"but sometimes everyone
has to have help."

I'll fly around
and look for a boat.
You be quiet. Just
rest there and float.

When you flop about
making waves everywhere,
I can't swim fast enough
to get up in the air."

Peppi Puffin huffed and puffed
and flapped his short wings.
(For the size of his body,
they are such little things.)

Oh, how he wished
to be a kittiwake or gull
with long slender wings,
and a body not so full.

His orange feet paddled
almost to the top,
but he fell back in the water
with an awkward plop.

"I am so streamlined
under the water.
I can swim like a fish
and dive like an otter.

Why can't I fly
to get help for this whale?
Away through the air
I will have to sail.

Woe is me.
How I do wish
I had not eaten
all those last fish!"

Peppi kept trying with
every ounce of his strength,
paddle, paddle went his feet,
his wings stretched full length.

Faster and faster his
frantic feet went
until with his
energy almost spent,
Peppi puffed,
"I must try harder."

And at last, at long last,
he was up in the air.
He began to circle and
search everywhere.

"What I must do
is look for a boat,
but not far out
where icebergs still float.

A sight-seeing boat is
what I must find,
with people on board
who are helpful and kind.

There are boats that
bring tourists out into the bay
that make several trips
all during the day."

Peppi flew in wide circles
the better to see
someone to help set
the troubled whale free.

"I'll fly back
toward the islands once more.
"Is that a boat I see,
over there near the shore?"

Peppi went closer
then dived with a swoop
and circled around
in a figure eight loop.

He zoomed full speed
over the pilot-house,
right past a lady
in a bright red blouse.

"What an odd looking bird.
Do you see?"
she cried. "Is it a duck?
What can it be?"

The boat pilot answered,
"That's a puffin.
They're called
'the Clowns of the Sea.'

He looked out the window
by the stool where he sat.
"But I've never seen a puffin
carry on like that."

Peppi kept swooping and
circling around,
all the time making
a loud puffin sound.

"If only I could speak
that strange people talk.
I try but all that comes
out is a squawk."

Peppi made one more dive
with all of his might,
then changed direction and
turned in his flight.

He fluttered his wings
and wiggled his tail,
then turned and flew back
toward the floundering whale.

He began to fly
straight out to sea.
"Now if only that boat
will just follow me."

"Did you see that,
when it turned to one side?
It looked like a signal,"
one person cried.

"Let's follow that bird and
see where it leads,"
the boat pilot said. "We'll find out
what that little bird needs."

Peppi's wings flapped as
fast as they could go,
while the faithful boat
putt-putted along down below.

He could see the whale now,
still leaping about,
but slower; it would
soon be tired out.

The boat pilot pointed.
"Look there to your right.
It's a breaching whale.
A spectacular sight!"

He steered the boat closer,
but not too near.
It would not be safe,
there was reason to fear.

They must stay a safe distance
away from the whale.
It could sink their small boat
with one flip of its tail.

"What can be wrong?"
Everyone wanted to know.
They could not tell
until the rope began to show.

"No wonder that poor whale
is so disturbed and upset.
It must have got tangled
in a fisherman's net."

"We will stay near.
We can do no more.
We must call for help.
I'll radio the shore.

Marine Animal Rescuers
live near the bay.
When a whale needs help
they will come right away."

Again and again the whale dived,
though not so deep;
then up out of the water,
but not so steep.

The watchers on the boat
couldn't help but admire
the whale's persistence
as it began to tire.

Peppi Puffin, too, was getting tired.
His feet felt like lead,
but the rescuers would watch
for a puffin overhead.

When they saw the puffin
flying high in the sky,
they would know the breaching whale
was somewhere nearby.

Peppi Puffin called to the
whale. "Help is coming.
They know what to do. You stay
quiet and let them help you."

(The danger of sea rescues
can be very chilling.
The crew cannot help
until the animal is willing.)

The whale stayed calm as
they came up to its head.
Nothing moved. It lay still
in its watery bed.

Only gasping breath could
be heard, a wheeze
that blew away
on the brisk sea breeze.

They still had to know
if the whale might take fright.
To see them so close
was a scary sight.

But right up to the huge head
one man went.
By looking in its eyes
he was confident;
he could tell the whale
was willing and ready.
It knew friends had come
and would be quiet and steady.

The team went to work.
One reached out with a clipper,
sliding it gently between
rope and flipper.

His arms were strong; the
sharp blades went snip, snip.
Several strands of the rope
were cut with each clip.

Carefully they worked
until the whale was free.
Soon it would be rested
and swim out to sea.

"HOORAY! HOORAY!
 for the daring, brave crew!
What a sight it was
to watch the team's rescue."

The tourists shouted with
a loud happy sound.
Peppi Puffin clapped his wings
and flew around and around.

The rescue team waved thanks
for all the acclaim,
then headed back to shore until
the next call for help came.

Animal rescues are dangerous,
each and every one,
but their best thanks come
from a job well done.

Another whale
had been saved.
The crew smiled to each other
as they waved.

Peppi relaxed on the water
near the exhausted whale.
"See?" he said. "Sometimes
help is needed before we can prevail."

He flew to a rock
above the waves of the bay.
"This has been
a most exciting day.

How happy I am to have
helped with this good deed.
Mama Puffin always said
we should help those in need."

Peppi waved good-by
as he flew away.
What a wonderful,
beautiful, joyful day.

Peppi sang to himself his favorite song:

"I'm Peppi Puffin, an Atlantic puffin,
we're called the Clowns of the Sea,
I am a happy, happy puffin
and so very glad to be me."

Acknowledgments:

Cover Photo & page 28 Photo Copyright © Henning Allmers

Title Page Photo, pages 3 & 47 photos Copyright © Henrik Thorburn

Page 1 Photo, Public Domain, www.pixabay.com

Page 2 Photo, Public Domain, www.public-domain-image.com

Page 5 Photo Copyright © Andrea Schaffer

Pages 6 & 32 Photos Copyright © Steve Garvie

Page 7 Photo Copyright © Oskar Elias Sorgurosson

Page 8 Photo Copyright © Paul Asman and Jill Lenoble

Page 9 Photo Copyright © John Edwards

Pages 10, 20, & 43 Photos Copyright © John H. Barnes

Pages 16, 17, 19, & 31 Photos, Public Domain,
www.freenaturepictures.com

Pages 21, 41, and 44 Photos, Public Domain from NOAA Library

Page 22 Photo Copyright © Hans Hillewaert

Page 24 Photo Copyright © Jorge Hempel

Pages 27 & 45 Photos Copyright © Andreas Trepte

Page 29 Photo Copyright © Marc Aubin

Page 30 Photo Copyright © John Goode

Page 33 Photo Copyright © Mark Medcalf

Page 35 Photo Copyright © Brian Summers

Page 37 Photo Copyright © Bar Harbor Whale Watch

Page 39 Photo Copyright © Matthew Hull

Page 40 Photo Copyright © Aleria Jensen, NOAA/NMFS/AKFSC

Page 42 Photo Copyright © Sorin Riise

Page 46 Photo from U.S. Fish and Wildlife Service – Northeast Region

Photos on pages 4, 11, 12, 13, 14, 15, 18, 23, 25, 26, 34, 36, & 38 were taken by the author

www.ingramcontent.com/pod-product-compliance
Lightning Source LLC
Chambersburg PA
CBHW041515280526
45792CB00004B/1256